A Williamson **W** *Tales Alive!*® Book

In The Days
OF
Dinosaurs

A Rhyming Romp Through Dino History

Howard Temperley

Illustrations by Michael Kline

Library of Congress Cataloging-in-Publication Data

Temperley, Howard.
    In the days of dinosaurs : a rhyming romp through
    dino history / written by Howard Temperley ;
    illustrations by Michael Kline.
            p. cm.
    "A Williamson tales alive book."
    ISBN 0-8249-8662-8 (pbk.)
    1. Dinosaurs—Juvenile poetry. 2. Children's poetry,
English. I. Kline, Michael P., ill. II. Title.

PR6120.E6515 2004
811'.6—dc22   2004040873

Tales Alive!® series editor: **Susan Williamson**
Project editor: **Emily Stetson**
Interior design: **Michael Kline**
Illustrations: **Michael Kline**
Cover design and illustration: **Michael Kline**

Published by Williamson Books
An imprint of Ideals Publications
A division of Guideposts
535 Metroplex Drive, Suite 250
Nashville, Tennessee 37211
800-586-2572

Printed in Italy
10 9 8 7 6 5 4 3 2 1

TO ANNABEL AND DANIEL BURNLEY,
FOR WHOM THESE VERSES
WERE ORIGINALLY WRITTEN

CONTENTS

When Dinosaurs Roamed the Earth

ong before my day and yours
The world was full of dinosaurs,
And where today our houses stand
Herds of them once roamed the land,
From east to west and north to south,
From mountaintop to river mouth,
Splashing about in river pools
Where now stand office blocks and schools,
Strutting about on springy legs,
Building nests and laying eggs,
From the Arctic Circle to Peru
And all around the equator, too.
On land and sea and in the air,
There were dinosaurs everywhere.

So as you sit and read this book
Just think how different it would look
If walls and windows, ceilings, floors,
Streets and cities, houses, doors,
And all the familiar things you know
Melted away like winter's snow.

And there, before your very eyes,
Were creatures of GIGANTIC size,
With lashing tails and massive jaws,
Spiky backs and crooked claws,
That waddled, hopped, and lumbered by
The places *we* now occupy,

As though this weird menagerie
Had just as much a right to be
Upon this earth as you and me,
Which makes me wonder what *they'd* say
About the world *we* have today.

MEET THE EARLY DINOS... & THEIR FRIENDS

The World of the Dinosaurs

**J**ust as we have mice and rats,
Sharks and whales, birds and bats,

Back in the Triassic age,
When dinosaurs first take the stage,

Reptiles of varying length and girth
Already thronged the sea and earth.

Some of them just crept about,
Half in the water and half out,

Catching insects, hunting around,
In lakes and ponds and on the ground.

Then, gradually, as time went by,
The more adventurous began to try

Running as birds and mammals do,
Some on four legs, some on two,

Acquiring along the way
Better teeth to catch their prey,

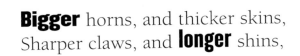

Bigger horns, and thicker skins,
Sharper claws, and **longer** shins,

And necks designed to help them feed;
While some grew **very large** indeed.

And so it was they came to be
The very creatures that you see

Illustrated in this book —
So turn the pages and have a look.

Scutosaurus
(scoo-too-SAWR-us)

 **his scutosaur** is a sorry sight,
I do not think it sleeps at night.
Its belly sags, its skin is slack,
It has a mountain on its back.
It looks as though its life's a bore.
I'm glad I'm not a scutosaur.

Lesothosaurus
(le-SOH-toh-SAWR-us)

This herbivore was very small
Being under two feet tall —
Or, putting it another way,
The size our turkeys are today.
Like them, it had two scaly feet,
Though whether it was as good to eat
The evidence does not reveal.
Still, it might have made a tasty meal
For allosaurs and megalosaurs
And other prowling carnivores.
Perhaps that's why it leaves the stage
Early in the Jurassic age.

Brachiosaurus
(BRAK-ee-o-SAWR-us)

 **ne of the biggest** beasts of all,
Brachiosaurus was so tall
It had the kind of head one sees
Bobbing over the tops of trees,
And as it slowly ambled round
Its mighty footsteps shook the ground.

But there were limits to the weight
Its slender neck could tolerate,
And as it needed teeth to chew,
A nose, and eyes, and ears, too,
The space remaining was so small
It had almost no brain at all.

Huge of body, small of brain,
A living, walking, mobile crane,
It spent its long and peaceful days
Doing nothing else but graze,
Often consuming, so they say,
Four hundred pounds of leaves a day,
Happily doing what it did best:
Bite ...
       Swallow ...
             And digest.

Barosaurus
(BAR-o-SAWR-us)

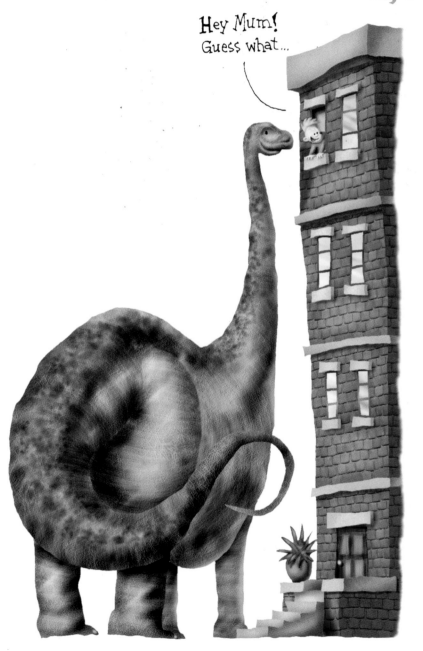

Hey Mum!
Guess what...

It is a pleasing
sight to see
A barosaur emerging
from the sea,
When what you took
to be a seal
Gradually approaches
to reveal
A neck and shoulders,
body, thighs,
Of quite an
astounding size.
A monster of
the Loch Ness sort,
It's longer than
a tennis court,
And well could look you
in the eye
Through a window
stories high.
A slow-moving,
harmless beast,
Its daily practice
is to feast
On ferns, plants,
and leafy sedge
That grow around
the water's edge,
And so it's often
to be found
In shallow waters
or marshy ground.

Diplodocus
(di-PLOD-o-kus)

iplodocus was seldom stirred
To leave the confines of the herd,

Thinking the thoughts that others thought
And doing the things that it was taught.

It ate the things that others ate,
And when they migrated would migrate,

Plodding along from day to day
In its own slow-motion way.

Diplodocus was, to say the least,
Rather a conformist beast.

Why Dinosaurs Swallowed Stones

s I believe I said before,
A fully grown brachiosaur
Was capable of putting away
Four hundred pounds of leaves a day.
So how, you wonder, did it turn
That soggy mass of leaves and fern,
And moss and twigs, and all the rest
Into a form it could digest?

Well, what these creatures did was find
So-called gastroliths to grind
What they had swallowed into a stew
The way our kitchen blenders do.
Thus, as they slowly ambled round
The stones inside them gently ground
That fibrous mass inside their bellies
Into digestible sorts of jellies.

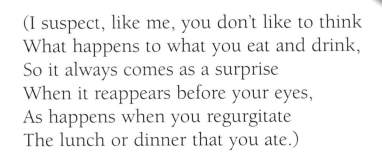

(I suspect, like me, you don't like to think
What happens to what you eat and drink,
So it always comes as a surprise
When it reappears before your eyes,
As happens when you regurgitate
The lunch or dinner that you ate.)

But returning to the brachiosaurs
And other large-scale herbivores —
The grinding stones were also meant
To help the churning mass ferment,
By which I simply mean to say
To help it all to rot away,
Creating heat internally,
Like the compost heaps you see.

You'd think it would have done them harm.
Instead, it helped to keep them warm,
The problem being all the gas
Created by that biomass.
Those herbivores, I fear, were not
Exactly a sweet-smelling lot.

On the Naming of Dinosaurs

**hen long ago** geologists found
Enormous fossils in the ground,
Not having seen the likes before
They coined the term "dinosaur."
("Terrifying lizard" in ancient Greek,
A language modern Greeks don't speak.)

Terrifying Lizard!

Once they'd started down that track,
There was, it seemed, no turning back.
And so we have gone on and wrung
From that long-abandoned tongue
Names that ordinary people find
Baffling to the tongue and mind
For the fossils that we try
To date, describe, and classify,
Names you'd find it hard to speak
Even if you *were* an ancient Greek,
Names like *Carcharodontosaurus*
(kar-KAR-oh-DON-toh-SAWR-us)
Or, even worse, *Incisivosaurus*
(in-SIGH-sih-vo-SAWR-us).

I wish that they had given thought
To the damage that they wrought
When they chose that language to
Convey their thoughts to me and you
And vowed in future to be sure
To choose a language less obscure.

Paleontologists
(PAL-ay-on-TOL-oh-gists)

Paleontologists are trained to see
Things unperceived by you and me,
And from a single piece of bone
Can reconstruct a skeleton.
They're also always finding more
Varieties of dinosaur,
And details, too, about the way
They lived their lives from day to day.

Yet there is much that even so
The greatest experts do not know,
For almost everything that is known
Comes from impressions left in stone,
That being all that's left today
Of the world that's passed away.

So what you see in dinosaur books
May tell you *something* about their looks,
But quite a lot of what you see
Is purely imaginary,
Like what the creatures' colors were.
Or whether they had scales or fur,
Artists being obliged to show
Lots of things we do not know.

Pterosaurs
(TER-o-SAWRS)

Pterosaurs were archosaurs,
Thus relatives of the dinosaurs,
Airborne cousins that would prey
On whatever came their way:
Mammals, birds, insects, slugs,
Fish and worms, flying bugs —
Scavengers prepared to eat
Practically any kind of meat.

Various in shape and size
They filled the prehistoric skies,
A menagerie of flying freaks:
Some with teeth and some with beaks,
In the air and on the ground,
Circling, flapping, pecking around,
Big and small, dull and bright,
Busying about in bat-like flight,
Behaving, in fact, in much the way
Our modern birds do today.

Pterodactylus
(TAIR-oh-DAK-til-us)

This creature's wings were strange affairs
Collapsible like canvas chairs,
Mostly made of bone and skin
With curious ways of folding in.

High above the Jurassic plains
They'd circle round like glider planes,
Or engage in aerial fights
Around their cliff-top nesting sites.

Out on the ocean, over the ground,
Zooming, gliding, flapping around,
Down in the valleys, high in the air,
You would see them everywhere.

Dinosaur Dream

 **I dreamed last night** that it was spring
And I heard the pterodactyls sing,

While the prehistoric trees
Echoed to their melodies.

The dinosaurs from far and near
Came flocking to the woods to hear

The enchanting notes cascade
So beautiful were the sounds they made.

And as the mighty cliffs around
Resonated to the sound,

Two by two in reel and rout,
All night long, they danced about.

Empires of the Sea

Just as pterodactyls flew,
Reptiles took to the oceans, too,
In time acquiring a weight and girth
Greater than those that stalked the earth,
As arms and legs became flippers and fins
And horny hides slippery skins.

(Just think how much that you could eat
If you dispensed with legs and feet
And didn't have to go to school —
Just floated in a swimming pool.)

And so, they grew to giant size,
With razor teeth and goblin eyes,
Behaving in a similar way
To the whales and dolphins of today.

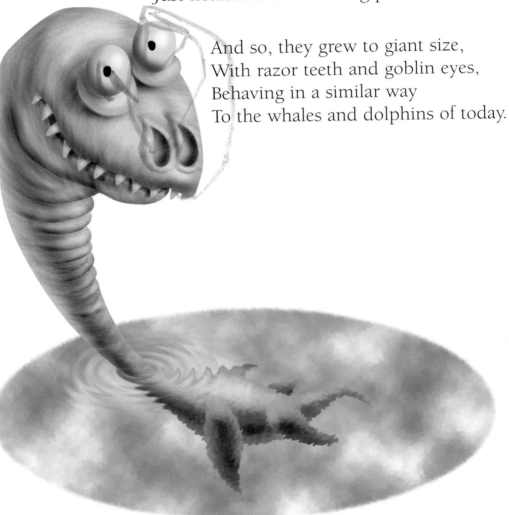

Liopleurodon
(LEE-oh-PLOO-ro-don)

This predatory giant
      Of the Jurassic seas
Could have swallowed you whole
      With the greatest of ease,
Though because it was armed
      With dagger-like teeth

That stuck out at angles
      Above and beneath,
If it wasn't too hungry
      And had time for the pleasure
It would probably have chosen
      To eat you at leisure.

WHEN DINOSAURS RULED THE EARTH

Incisivosaurus
(in-SIGH-sih-vo-SAWR-us)

he oddest ever dinosaur
Is the incisivosaur.
It looks as if its various bits
Came from different construction kits:
A chicken's feet, a raptor's claws,
A magpies' tail, a woodchuck's jaws.
But the thing that really makes it funny,
Are two front teeth just like Bugs Bunny.

Caudipteryx
(kaw-DIP-ter-iks)

he *Caudipteryx* is a freak
With scales, feathers, and a beak.
Reptile, dinosaur, or bird?
Appearance-wise it's quite absurd,
Which makes you think it didn't know
In what direction it should go.

How Dinosaurs Learned to Fly

f dinos were (as we have heard)
The ancestors of the modern bird,
You well may wonder how and why
Such earthbound creatures learned to fly.
Well, one thing they plainly *didn't* do,
And that was think the whole thing through.
They didn't sit down to figure out
What flying was really all about,
Using brain-power in the way
Our engineers do today.
Their brains just didn't help one bit —
Thinking had *nothing* to do with it.

So growing wings was not a sign
Of their well-thought-out design,
But simply the way that creatures strive
From day to day to stay alive,
Flying being a useful way
Of finding food and hunting prey.

But gliding has its uses, too,
When enemies are after you
Jumping from branches to get away
Like the flying squirrels of today
Who flit about among the trees
And leap great distances with ease.

Wings will also help you bound
More rapidly along the ground
As farmyard hens and ducklings do
And ostriches and emus, too.

Hey!

And so, by incremental stages,
Gradually through the ages,
As some lived and others died
The better flyers multiplied,
Eventually turning, so some say,
Into the birds we have today.

Microraptor
(MY-krow-RAP-tore)

lthough it may look very cute
This mini-dino is a brute,

So if you're looking for a pet
This is one you'd best forget.

Its teeth are sharp, its claws the same;
It is quite impossible to tame.

I'd find a pet with nicer habits —
Why not guinea pigs and rabbits?

Velociraptor
(vee-LOSS-ih-RAP-tor)

**his theropod** is very fit;
You'd have a job escaping it.
Its legs are sinewy and strong,
Its stride's exceptionally long,
And when it's hunting with a pack
It twists and turns and doubles back
With outstretched tail and open jaws,
Springy gait and razor claws.
Supple, agile, fast, and lean,
It is a dangerous machine.

Raptors Always Chewed Their Food

Whatever raptors caught for food,

When they ate, they always chewed.

You may have heard the Bible tale

How Jonah was swallowed by a whale,

But that whale quite plainly failed to chew

The way your parents tell you to,

And so was unable to digest

Its celebrated human guest.

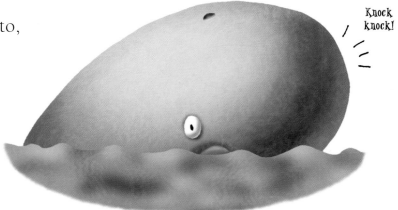

Knock knock!

But had a raptor
     got hold of him,
The story would have
     been quite grim.
For when a raptor
     grabs onto you
Its natural instinct
     is to chew.
Now let's not make
     too much of it,
But it would chew you
     bit by bit,
Using its molars
     to crack your bones,
Regardless of
     your shrieks and moans,
Pausing briefly
     to lick its lips
Before getting down
     to your spine and hips,
And when it's reduced you
     to a pulp,
It'll swallow you down,
    gulp
       by
         gulp.

Raptors

knew

to

masticate

every

mouthful

that

they

ate

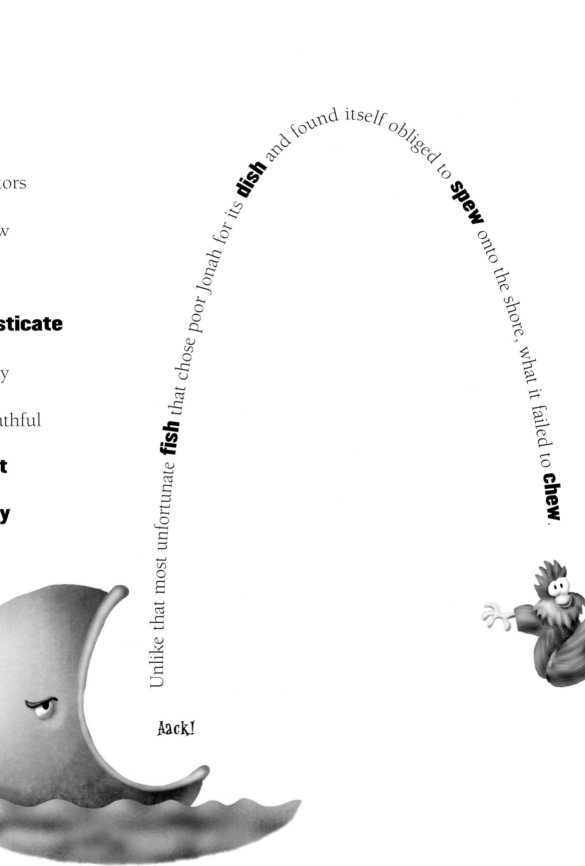

Aack!

Unlike that most unfortunate **fish** that chose poor Jonah for its **dish** and found itself obliged to **spew** onto the shore, what it failed to **chew**.

Carcharodontosaurus
(kar-KAR-oh-DON-toh-SAWR-us)

his creature gives a toothy smile
Rather like a crocodile,
As it daily welcomes in
Fur and feather, scale and fin,
Grateful for whatever fate
Happens to put upon its plate.
But isn't it an awful shame
They gave the creature such a name?

Urp!

Styracosaurus
(sty-RACK-o-SAWR-us)

You very well may wonder how
A sort of prehistoric cow —
Whose principal concerns
Were eating leaves, moss, and ferns
Or sleeping on a sunny bank —
Developed armor like a tank.

It seems meat-eating dinosaurs
Preyed on the styracosaurs.
But styracosaurs with stronger backs
Were able to ward off attacks,
And so were those with horny hides
That helped them to protect their sides.

So as the thin-skinned ones all died
Only thick-skinned ones survived,
Becoming heavier by stages,
Gradually throughout the ages,
Till in the end they grew so stout
That they could scarcely walk about,
And finally they came to be
This fearsome creature that you see.

Parasaurolophus
(PAIR-ah-SAWR-oh-LOAF-us)

No creature had a louder roar
Than this crested dinosaur,
Its nasal passages being a type
Of resonating organ pipe
So remarkably long and wide
A full-grown man could stand inside.

In the North America of their day
You'd hear them honking miles away,
Much as you hear freight trains do
And fog-bound coastal steamers, too.

Was the aim to communicate
At a distance with a mate?
Or were those ear-splitting roars
Meant to scare off predators?
As often, scientists disagree,
But this much seems quite clear to me:
Even before the human race
America was a noisy place.

Troodon
(TROH-oh-don)

Quick of mind and sharp of sight
Troodon hunted day and night,
Running around on scaly feet
Seeking out small game to eat —
Birds and lizards, mice and voles —
Up in trees, down in holes,
Listening for the slightest sound,
Peering, pausing, sniffing around.

Not quite a lizard, not quite a bird,
Partly feathered, partly furred,
It used its speed to catch its prey.
How fast it was I cannot say,
But of all the theropods of its day
Troodon would be the one
That I would put my money on.

Euoplocephalus
(YEW-oh-ploh-SEFF-a-lus)

uoplocephalus has a tail
It uses as a sort of flail

Ending in a heavy ball,
Like wreckers use to smash a wall.

If approached, it will spin around
And knock you smartly to the ground.

Tortoise-like, it has sheath
Protecting what is underneath.

The spines you see along its back
Are there to ward off an attack.

Generally a placid beast,
Its normal practice is to feast

Like cows and other ruminants
On vegetables and broad-leafed plants.

Providing that you don't go near
You need not have a cause for fear.

Oviraptor
(OH-vih-RAP-tor)

The ***Oviraptor**** — one of nature's pests —
Lives by robbing others' nests,
Which means it's constantly at war
With every other dinosaur.
In spite of which its step is light,
Its beak is sharp, its eyes are bright,
Giving it a jaunty air,
Artful, roguish, debonair.

Like criminals of the professional sort,
It sees thievery as a sport,
A game of patience, wit, and daring
Quite devoid of moral bearing
That leaves the successful robber feeling
Superior to those from whom it's stealing.

It doesn't even *kill* its prey,
Just steals their eggs and runs away,
Legging it to some retreat,
Where it can safely pause to eat,
Which takes a lot of nerve to do
When foes are bigger far than you.
Its eye is sharp, its brain is cunning,
It is exceptionally good at running.
But, if *T. rex* were after you,
You'd need to learn to run fast, too!

*When scientists first discovered the fossils of the *Oviraptor*, the dino's fossils were surrounded by fossilized eggs, which the scientists believed to be *Oviraptor's* food. Thus, they named the dino *Oviraptor*, which means "egg thief." Scientists now believe those egg fossils may have been the *Oviraptor's* own eggs that it was protecting, much like our brooding hens do today!

Tyrannosaurus rex
(ti-RAN-o-SAWR-us rex)

Tyrannosaurus likes to eat
Large amounts of tasty meat.
Being such a greedy beast
It's always ready for a feast,
And will happily devour
Smaller creatures by the hour.
It charges down upon its prey
Before they've time to run away,
And, raising its enormous head,
Shakes its victims till they're dead.
Although it has a tiny brain,
It's faster than a railway train.
I do not think I'd like to meet
Tyrannosaurus in the street.

Ankylosaurus
(ANG-kill-oh-SAWR-us)

 *nkylosaurus* has a leathery hide
With rows of spikes along the side,
Also a tail with which to whack
Enemies that might attack.
What predator would seek to make a feast
Of such a heavily armored beast?

Dinosaurs Weren't Very Bright

Dinosaurs weren't very bright,
They never learned to read or write
Or multiply five by ten
Or even how to hold a pen.

Their main concern was eating meals
Rather than inventing wheels,
Or any of the useful things
Scientific progress brings.

Had they aimed a little higher,
They might have learned to light a fire,
Which goes to show it's not enough
To hang around, playing tough.

Triceratops
(try-SER-a-tops)

ehold this ugly quadruped,
The weight of bone upon its head,
Its horny beak, its carapace,
The grim expression on its face,
Its triple horns, its massive frill —
You can't deny it's dressed to kill.
Those three-foot horns upon its pate
Would punch a hole in armor plate.
A helmet's useful in a fight,
But would you wear one day and night?
Imagine having to go to bed
With all that junk upon your head!

A Word from Dino Foods, Inc.

What made the dinosaurs big and strong
Enabling them to live so long?
How come pterosaurs flew so high
They were invisible to the naked eye?
They didn't bother with junk food,
They ate the things that did them good —
Organic vegetables and meats,
Not nasty drinks and sticky sweets.
They had no use for dentists' drills,
Hospitals, or doctors' pills
Because they all led healthy lives
With lots of fresh-air exercise.
They did the things that they should do,
And, doctors tell us, *so should you.*
So why not go ahead and try it?
     Give yourself
       A DINO DIET!

THE END OF THE AGE OF DINOSAURS

The Death of the Dinosaurs

**nd so**, they lived from day to day,
Eating ferns or hunting prey,
Supposing that the world was theirs
For near two hundred million years,
Never thinking that one day
They would all be swept away.

Meanwhile, out
    in distant space,
The asteroid that
    would end their race,*
A rock of quite
    enormous girth,
Was homing in
    on Mother Earth,
Coming closer
    year by year
Till, arcing through
    the atmosphere,
A blinding streak
    of fiery light,
It struck the earth with
    all the might
Of megatons
    of dynamite.

*There are also other theories as to what caused
the dinosaurs to disappear from the earth.

The sky turned black;
    the trees grew bare.
Volcanic ashes
    filled the air.
It grew so dark
    you could not say
What was night
    and what was day
Or even what
    the seasons were
As winter lasted
    all the year.

The creatures that

Had roamed around

Fell and perished

On the ground,

So when at last

The skies all cleared,

The dinosaurs

Had disappeared,

Leaving only

Piles of bones

That gradually

Turned into stones.

Let us hope

That one day we

Don't perish quite

So miserably!

Dinosaur Nightmare

**ave you ever** lain in dread
Of something underneath your bed?
Have you awoken from a dream
And found yourself too scared to scream,
Not even daring to take a breath
Because you were so scared to death?
Have you feared to turn and see
What sort of creature it might be —
That scaly beast with crooked claws
Climbing up your chest of drawers —
Or to look at that enormous head
Gazing down upon your bed?

Of course, it's just a silly dream;
Things are seldom what they seem,
Especially very late at night
When you awaken in a fright.

Dinosaurs are dead and gone;
Time has claimed them, every one.
It may be that beneath your bed
Lie silent empires of the dead,
Relics of that time gone by
When lizards ruled the earth and sky.
But if they *are* beneath your bed
Just remember: *They are dead!*

So how could they come crawling out,
First a claw and then a snout,
Writhing up from beneath the ground,
Shaking themselves and running around?
Besides, I doubt they'd do you harm.
So there's no cause for alarm.

But wait!
Did you hear that rumbling sound,
Of something moving underground?
Am I making a mistake
Or has the house begun to shake?
What's that coming down the lane
And peering through the windowpane?
What's moving underneath the floor?
What's that thumping at the door?
I'm sure you have no cause for fear,
But that heavy breathing that I hear
Sounds as if it's rather near,
Something with a scaly skin,
Something
                    that is
                              coming in!

Fossils

Most animals of which we know
Became extinct so long ago
The only traces to be found
Are buried far beneath the ground.
Showing us how, bit by bit,
Nature deals with the unfit,
Consigning to oblivion
Those it chooses, one by one,
Gradually, year by year,
Till whole species disappear.

Across the prairies and the plains
Lie their fossilized remains,
And under cities where at night
Buildings are ablaze with light,
Down beneath their paving stones
Layer on layer lie their bones.
Subject all to Nature's laws,
Carnivores and herbivores,
Those that caught and ate their prey
And those that simply ran away,
Fierce or timid, big or small,
Mother Earth embraced them all.

After the Dinosaurs

The fossil record, sad to say,
Is all that's left of them today.
And yet, it was a stroke of luck,
At least for us, that asteroid struck.
For with the tyrant lizards gone
Other creatures, one by one,
Dormice, shrews, weasels, voles,
Emerging from their hiding holes,
Little creatures of the night
That would sooner flee than fight,
Gradually found that they
Could venture out by light of day
And so in time took the place
Of that vanished reptile race.

And so it was this motley crew
Starting out on life anew
Grew in weight and height and girth
And spread themselves around the earth.
And thus the world began to grow
Far more like the world you know,
With lions and tigers, dogs and cats,
Cows and horses, mice and rats,
Some of which began to learn
How to be tyrants in their turn,
Including the one I have to call
The greatest predator of all!

What was it that made all others quail?
Was it the giant killer whale?
Some Ice Age beast with lots of hair?
The great white shark? The grizzly bear?
Some creature of gigantic size
With gaping jaws and scary eyes?
The dire wolf of Kurdistan?
No. The greatest predator is *MAN*.

The Wonder of It All

**on't you wish** that you could go
Back to that world of long ago
Of tyrannosaurs and hadrosaurs
And all those other dinosaurs?
They lived their lives from day to day
(Which seemed to them the normal way)
Because, unlike me and you,
That was all that they could do:
Never pausing to reflect,
Because they lacked our intellect.

Being more informed than they
We look at things a different way,
Knowing the world before our eyes
Was long ago quite otherwise.
So what a shame we couldn't be
Actually around to see
The marvel of that vanished age
When giant reptiles walked the stage.

But in this century and the last
We've learned a lot about the past,
Allowing us, at this late date,
Finally to appreciate —
Although it's gone beyond recall —
The sheer wonder of it all.

DINOSAUR TIME LINE

(mya=million years ago)

Dinosaurs ruled the land for more than 160 million years, from about 228 million years ago (mya) to 65 million years ago. Scientists call this time the *Mesozoic Era*. They divide it into three periods: the *Triassic*, the *Jurassic*, and the *Cretaceous*. During the *Mesozoic Era*, things on earth changed drastically, from being one large continent called *Pangaea* (pan-JE-a) to becoming just about the shape the continents are today. A lot was going on back then! Take a look and find the dinos in this book and their friends.

MESOZOIC ERA ("Middle Life") 250 to 65 mya

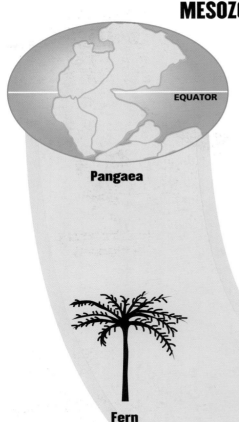

Pangaea

EQUATOR

The Triassic Period (250 to 205 mya)

At the beginning of the Triassic Period, all the continents were joined together in a huge, single "supercontinent" called Pangaea near the equator. The weather was very hot, with dry deserts at the center of the continent and tropical areas at the coasts. Much of the vegetation consisted of giant ferns and tall primitive conifer trees. There were many earthquakes and lots of volcanic activity. Dinosaurs began to appear and take the stage.

Fern

Conifer

Lesothosaurus (about 225 to 200 mya)

Scutosaurus (250 mya)

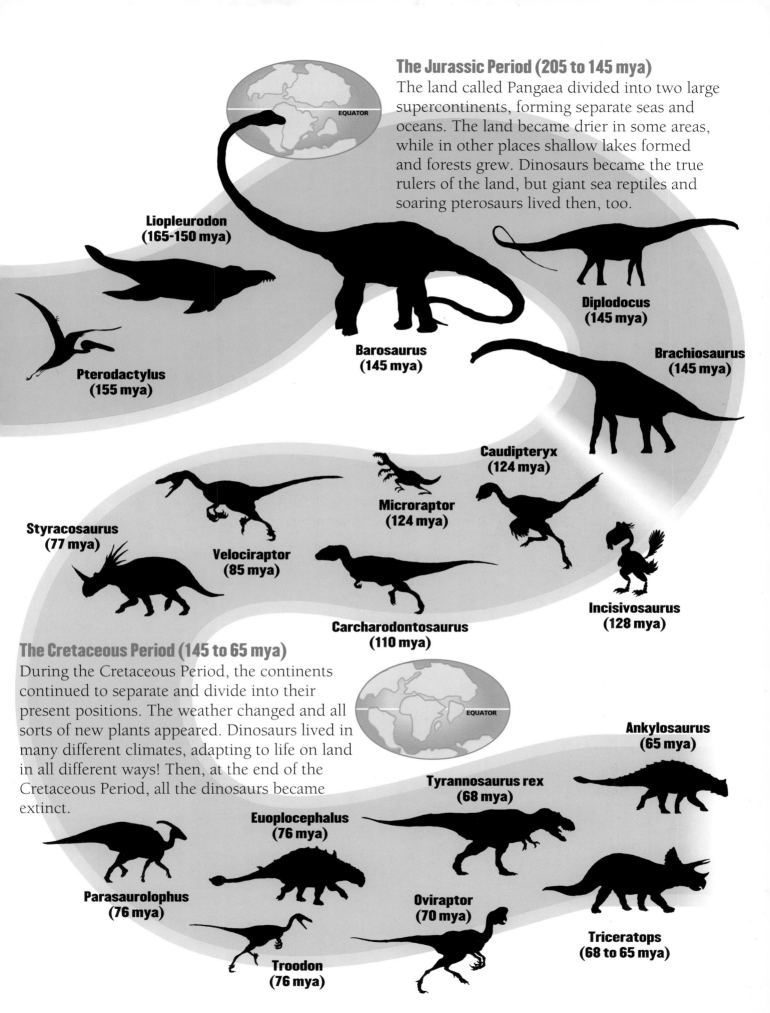

The Jurassic Period (205 to 145 mya)

The land called Pangaea divided into two large supercontinents, forming separate seas and oceans. The land became drier in some areas, while in other places shallow lakes formed and forests grew. Dinosaurs became the true rulers of the land, but giant sea reptiles and soaring pterosaurs lived then, too.

EQUATOR

Liopleurodon
(165-150 mya)

Diplodocus
(145 mya)

Barosaurus
(145 mya)

Brachiosaurus
(145 mya)

Pterodactylus
(155 mya)

Caudipteryx
(124 mya)

Microraptor
(124 mya)

Styracosaurus
(77 mya)

Velociraptor
(85 mya)

Incisivosaurus
(128 mya)

Carcharodontosaurus
(110 mya)

The Cretaceous Period (145 to 65 mya)

During the Cretaceous Period, the continents continued to separate and divide into their present positions. The weather changed and all sorts of new plants appeared. Dinosaurs lived in many different climates, adapting to life on land in all different ways! Then, at the end of the Cretaceous Period, all the dinosaurs became extinct.

EQUATOR

Ankylosaurus
(65 mya)

Tyrannosaurus rex
(68 mya)

Euoplocephalus
(76 mya)

Parasaurolophus
(76 mya)

Oviraptor
(70 mya)

Triceratops
(68 to 65 mya)

Troodon
(76 mya)

More *Great Books* from Williamson Books!

If you like to read stories, craft, create, and keep busy with fun things to do, we have some great books for you. All of these books are for people aged 8 and over, contain 120 to 144 pages, are printed in one- or two-color, are full-sized trade paperbacks (8½ x 11, 11 x 8½, 10 x 10), unless otherwise noted.

Benjamin Franklin Best Multicultural Book Award
TALES OF THE SHIMMERING SKY
Ten Global Folktales with Activities
by Susan Milord
Full-color original art, $14.95

Storytelling World Honor Award
BIRD TALES
From Near and Far
by Susan Milord
Full-color original art, 96 pages, $14.95.

Kids' Easy-to-Create WILDLIFE HABITATS
for Small Spaces in City, Suburbs, Countryside
by Emily Stetson, $12.95

Parents' Choice Honor Award
THE KIDS' NATURAL HISTORY BOOK
Making Dinos, Fossils, Mammoths & More
by Judy Press, $12.95

Benjamin Franklin Best Juvenile Fiction Award
TALES ALIVE!
Ten Multicultural Folktales with Activities
by Susan Milord
Full-color original art, $14.95

Parents' Choice Gold Award
THE KIDS' MULTICULTURAL ART BOOK
Art & Craft Experiences from Around the World
by Alexandra M. Terzian, $12.95

Parents' Choice Gold Award
THE KIDS' NATURE BOOK
365 Indoor/Outdoor Activities & Experiences
by Susan Milord, $12.95

Parents' Choice Honor Award
MONARCH MAGIC!
Butterfly Activities & Nature Discoveries
by Lynn M. Rosenblatt
Ages 4–12, 96 pages, more than 100 full-color photos, 8 x 10, $12.95

Dr. Toy 10 Best Socially Responsible Products
MAKE YOUR OWN BIRDHOUSES & FEEDERS
by Robyn Haus, 64 pages, $8.95

Teachers' Choice Award
GEOLOGY ROCKS!
50 Hands-On Activities to Explore the Earth
by Cindy Blobaum, 96 pages, $12.95

GREAT GAMES!
Ball, Board, Quiz & Word,
Indoors & Out, for Many or Few!
by Sam Taggar, $12.95

Selection of Book-of-the-Month; Scholastic Book Clubs
KIDS COOK!
Fabulous Food for the Whole Family
by Sarah Williamson and Zachary Williamson, $12.95

Children's Book Council Notable Social Studies Trade Book
WHO REALLY DISCOVERED AMERICA?
Unraveling the Mystery & Solving the Puzzle
by Avery Hart, $12.95

GARDEN FUN!
Indoors & Out; In Pots & Small Spots
by Vicky Congdon, 64 pages, $7.95

40 KNOTS TO KNOW
Hitches, Loops, Bends & Bindings
by Emily Stetson, 64 pages, $8.95

Parents' Choice Silver Honor Award
Awesome OCEAN SCIENCE!
Investigating the Secrets of the Underwater World
by Cindy A. Littlefield, $12.95

Parents' Choice Recommended
The Kids' Guide to FIRST AID
All About Bruises, Burns, Stings, Sprains & Other Ouches
by Karen Buhler Gale, R.N., $12.95

REAL-WORLD MATH for Hands-On Fun!
by Cindy A. Littlefield, $12.95

THE KIDS' WILDLIFE BOOK
Exploring Animal Worlds Through Indoor/Outdoor Experiences
by Warner Shedd, $12.95

Visit Our Website!

To see what's new at Williamson and at Ideals Publications, and to learn more about specific books, visit our website at:
www.williamsonbooks.com

To Order Books:
Toll-free phone orders with any major credit card:
1-800-586-2572
Or, send a check with your order to:
Williamson Books
535 Metroplex Drive,
Nashville, TN 37211
For a free catalog: mail, phone, or fax **(888-815-2759)**

Please add **$4.00** for postage for one book plus **$1.00** for each additional book. Satisfaction is guaranteed or full refund without questions or quibbles.

Thank you.

Williamson Books is an imprint of Ideals Publications, a division of Guideposts.